Contents

FUN ACTIVITIES

ADIRONDACK
for Kids and Families
EXPLORATION
History, Discovery & Fun!

MELINDA MACKESEY

Charleston London

THE
History
PRESS

Published by The History Press
Charleston, SC 29403
www.historypress.net

First published 2011

Manufactured in the United States

ISBN 978.1.60949.498.8
Library of Congress Cataloging-in-Publication Data
Mackesey, Melinda H.
Adirondack exploration for kids and families : history, discovery and
fun / Melinda H. Mackesey.
p. cm.
ISBN 978-1-60949-498-8
1. Adirondack Mountains (N.Y.)--History. 2. Adirondack Mountains
(N.Y.)--Description and travel. 3. Adirondack Mountains (N.Y.)--Social
life and customs. 4. Natural history--New York (State)--Adirondack
Mountains. 5. Family recreation--New York (State)--Adirondack
Mountains. 6. Creative activities and seat work. I. Title.
F127.A2M29 2011
974.7'5--dc23
2011042014

Notice: The information in this book is true and complete to the best
of our knowledge. It is offered without guarantee on the part of the
author or The History Press. The author and The History Press
disclaim all liability in connection with the use of this book.

Chapter 1

The Adirondack Landscape

The Adirondack Mountain range located in upstate New York is situated south of the Canadian border, north of the Mohawk River, west of Lake Champlain and east of the St. Lawrence River. The park encompasses six million acres; 60 percent of those acres is owned privately, while the remaining 40 percent is owned by the people of the State of New York. The Adirondack Mountains' massive size in the number of total acres would cover all the national parks of Yosemite, Yellowstone, Glacier, Grand Canyon and the Great Smoky Mountains combined. Within the Adirondack Mountain range, the Department of Environmental Conservation has estimated that there are over thirty thousand miles of streams, 2,800 lakes and ponds and forty-three mountain peaks whose summits reach more than four thousand feet above sea level. Glacier activity has been attributed to forming the area's large number of ponds and lakes, as well as

View at the top of Crane Mountain. This April hike offered a different look at the mountains; without the leaf covering, you get to see the landscape contours. A few snow and ice patches are still visible in the nearby landscape.

giving the majority of the mountains their rounded-over appearance, scattered display and rolling contour. The Adirondack Mountains are associated with Canada's Laurentian Mountains, not the Appalachian Mountains. Due to the area's steep terrain, generally poor, rocky soil and short growing season, this region did not experience a great population growth like the rest of the country during the mid-1800s. With the exception of early times, when heavy logging and mining occurred, most of the Adirondacks remain as much wilderness as when Lewis Evans first explored the region and wrote about the area as "drowned impassable lands." Today, the Adirondack Park is protected by New York State's constitution as a park, "forever kept as wild forest land."

Year	National Park	Acres
1872	Yellowstone	2,219,789
1890	Yosemite	761,266
1910	Glacier	1,013,572
1919	Grand Canyon	1,217,403
1939	Great Smoky National Park	521,086
Total		**5,733,116**

SPOTLIGHT ON: ELEVATION

Elevation largely determines the plant and tree growth in the Adirondack Mountains. Certain plant species found in the Adirondacks today were amazingly here some four thousand years ago. As elevation increases, temperature decreases, and only certain plants survive at these colder temperatures. A 300-foot rise in elevation can drop the areas temperature by one degree Fahrenheit. On a sunny summer day in August, the temperature in Lake Placid Village was eighty-six degrees, but when we reached the top of Whiteface Mountain, with an elevation of 4,610 feet, the temperature was fifty-eight degrees.

Higher elevation conditions offer barren, thinner soils on mountain slopes, making the higher-elevation soils a suitable host for black spruce, balsam fir, red spruce, big tooth aspen and paper birch. This forest community can be found at elevations of 2,800 to 3,000 feet. The mountain slope's soil here can be very thin, acidic and nutrient-poor. The highest-elevation plants grow only up to the height of

Above: Glacial ice scraped soils from the Adirondack peaks. Here, exposed rock surfaces are partially covered in mosses, lichens or other alpine plants.

Opposite: View from Whiteface Mountain, 4,867 feet high. Hike the trail or drive up the Whiteface Memorial Highway for a 360-degree view. On a clear day, glimpses of Canada and Vermont topography can be spotted. The peak also has a castle, an elevator shaft for easy access and a weather station.

the annual snow depths (alpine habitat, heath plants). Ice storms, coupled with relentless winds, shear off anything above the snow levels.

Trees more suited for lower-elevation conditions include the white cedar, sugar maple, hemlock, white pine, American beech, red oak, yellow birch and tamarack. Soils that attract these trees are generally deeper, hold more moisture, have better drainage and are more fertile than the higher-elevation soils.

9

SPOTLIGHT ON: QUAGMIRES

Quagmire, bog or fens are all terms to describe a variety of soggy wetland environments. Their formation occurred as glacial activity buried large ice blocks that were forcefully pressed into the earth's surface.

These waterlogged areas are frequently found in regions of the Northern Hemisphere, like the Adirondacks, where year-round climate offers cool, moist temperatures and plentiful yearly precipitation. These areas play a crucial role in maintaining an ecological balance, soaking up excess water during seasonal snowmelts and rains and preventing water runoff and erosion, while in summer months these same wetlands slowly release their stored water supply.

Bogs are wetlands that make their own soil called peat. The bogs were formed thousands of years ago as ancient glacier movement dug deep holes into the Adirondacks' soil. Peat layers are made of partially decomposed plant and animal life. The buildup of sediment mixture includes sphagnum moss, leather leaf and other partially decayed plant matter accumulating over the years. Usually, a floating carpet of intertwined roots and plants of the sphagnum moss and leather leaf encompasses the bog.

Classified as ombrogenous, these wetlands have no water inlet or outlet, instead getting their waters from nutrient-lacking precipitation. Bogs have high-acidic waters, with levels very similar to that of tomato juice, PH range 3.0–4.0. These levels are due to nutrient-poor surrounding soils

This beaver dam floods existing trees and agriculture lands. The dam creates a pond with suitable water depths to protect the beavers' lodge from predator invasion.

and oxygen-deprived waters. As a result, bogs are not a favorable host to expected animal and plant wetland life. They are, however, loved by scientists, as they are very old and provide valuable insight in understanding the climate, vegetation and wildlife changes of the past as the scientists analyze the layers of peat buildup.

Fun Activity!
North Woods XIV Article

The answer can be found in section XIV, Article of the New York State Constitution (and on page 84).

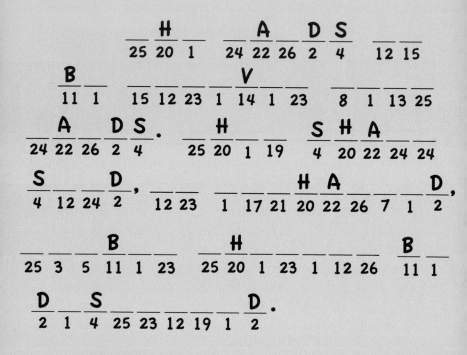

A	B	C	D	E	F	G	H	I	J	K	L
22	11		2				20				

M	N	O	P	Q	R	S	T	U	V	W	X	Y	Z
						4			14				

```
 _  H  _        S  _  A  _  _          S  H  A  _  _
25 20  1        4 25 22 25  1          4 20 22 24 24

 A  S  _  _  _  D            _  _  _  _  S  _
22  4 18  3 24  2           15 12 23  1  4 25

 _  _  _        B  _          _  _  A  S  _  D ,
26 12 25       11  1         24  1 22  4  1  2

 _  _  _        S  H  A  _  _          _  _  H  _
26 12 23        4 20 22 24 24         25 20  1

 S  _  _  D ,          _  _  _  _  _  V  _  D ,        _  _
 4 12 24  2           23  1  5 12 14  1  2            12 23
```

Chapter 2

Nature in the Adirondacks

When you walk through the woods, smell the fragrance of the nearby evergreens and feel the cushion of their needles under your shoes. These are just some of the aesthetic values nature gives us. In visiting the Adirondack Park, always look for the ways the natural world is interconnected. Each creature can affect and be affected by the other's actions. By exploring nature through hiking or canoeing activities, we can become more aware that we are stewards of the earth. As such, our existence is dependent on a healthy earth to provide us with clean air, clean water and nourishing vegetation. Those essential elements are just as necessary to the summer grasshopper, the black bear or the eastern white pine tree.

Having a state park safeguards lands in their natural form for future enjoyment. The aesthetic benefits the Adirondack Park provides are opportunities for recreation, pleasant views, wildlife habitat, water supply

A dragonfly at Ferd's Bog, which is located in the Pigeon Lake Wilderness, Eagle Bay, New York. This quick .3-mile hike has great wetland viewing on a floating plastic decking reaching into the bog's middle.

and natural flooding management. In the United States, many communities are struggling to preserve farmlands, wetlands, forests and parks. It is the lifelong struggle between two forces: those concerned with the natural ecosystem v. those concerned with human economic growth. In 1885, the people of the state of New York legislatively voted to protect and conserve the Adirondacks, along with its natural resources within the park, in order to minimize impact on the natural ecosystems.

Spotlight On: H_2O

H_2O: water by another name. The Adirondack topography and elevation create the perfect formula for lots of snow and rainfall each year. The surface depressions formed years ago by glacier action capture rain and snow.

The water cycle has three essential parts: precipitation, evaporation and condensation. The precipitation that falls on the Adirondacks is captured and stored by the abundant rich mosses, which slowly release the supply to the plants or provide runoff to rivers and lakes.

Lake Pleasant looking toward Oak Mountain on a July morning bike ride along South Shore Road.

A one-hundred-year-old nineteenth-century guide boat on display at Camp Santanoni's boathouse. These boats were preferred by Adirondack guides for their lightweight construction, coupled with their capacity to hold sportsmen and their gear.

The cycle continues as water reenters the atmosphere by transpiration and evaporation. Water taken in through the plants' root systems goes up the stem to the leaf. Then the tiny pores in the plants' leaves release water vapor back into the atmosphere as the plants release oxygen, a process called transpiration.

Another process in which water reenters the atmosphere can easily be observed on a sunny summer morning as the daybreak mist rises off a lake. The steam-like vapor rising to the atmosphere is caused by the sun's energy, causing water to evaporate from the lake's surface. That vapor is carried by warm air currents, cooling as it rises. It turns into tiny water droplets and attaches to other droplets, eventually forming clouds. As the air cools, it condenses into droplets that fall to the earth as rain (precipitation).

The water-storing power of the Adirondacks' numerous bogs, lakes and streams create a vast water reservoir for New York State. Mountain streams feed the state's larger waterways, maintaining adequate water levels throughout the seasons.

Spotlight On: Natural Selection

Life in the Adirondack wilderness is a struggle for existence as each species fiercely competes for the same limited supplies of food, shelter and water while enduring harsh climates and evading predator dangers. Those living creatures unable of adapting to the surroundings struggle, become weaker, die and ultimately become extinct. Stronger species having characteristics more suited to survival will live to reproduce offspring having their parents' survival traits. Those less adaptive will diminish in numbers.

The main focus of the theory of **natural selection** is that the natural environment is the selecting agent. Species possessing genetic qualities more suited for surviving in the environmental conditions at that time are more likely to survive to maturity. The more enduring species will produce

On walks, take photos of some of your favorite discoveries. This bright orange mushroom was noticed on the trail before Ferd's Bog.

offspring. Those species with less favorable characteristics to persevere will die. Nature selects the species best at adapting to their changing environments, leaving behind stronger, more successful species to populate the land.

The concept of natural selection was first published by Charles Darwin in his 1859 book, *The Origin of Species*, giving a scientific explanation to the theory of evolution. Darwin did this by providing scientific evidence from his more than thirty years of observing, collecting and researching nature's data and then documenting the differences in animal species, as well as the extinction of others.

Fossils are the historic proof, or footprint, of life forms that lived long ago that no longer exist today. Fossils of trilobites, clams and other marine organisms expose that a shallow ocean at one time covered New York State and part of the Adirondacks. These extinct creatures are believed to have been destroyed by either slow environmental changes or by catastrophic events such as volcanic eruptions, meteor strikes or widespread flooding.

Today, certain extinct populations can be tied to human activity past or present, including agricultural practices, hunting, forest destruction and the loss of open spaces. Species extirpated by hunting and trapping include the gray wolf, mountain lion, panther, wolverine, beaver, elk and moose. These animals were killed because they provided man with a source of income. Some of these animals were killed as early settlers protected their domestic stock. The reduction of birds of prey like the peregrine falcon, hawk and eagle can be explained by the agricultural industry's use of the pesticide DDT. Yet human activity, good or bad, can be said to be part of the natural selection process. Man has also reversed past damages to endangered species by passing laws that protect habitats, ban trapping, limit hunting, restrict the use of certain pesticides and regulate causes of acid rain.

SPOTLIGHT ON: BEAVERS

The **beaver** is the official mammal of New York State and makes its home in the Adirondacks. Beavers are the largest North American rodent, and although they are not nocturnal, they are generally busiest at dusk. Beavers are expert builders of dams and lodges whose main tools are their large incisor teeth that continue to grow throughout the animal's life. Another unique tool is the beaver's transparent eyelids, allowing clear underwater vision. The dams and lodges they build are made of mud, stones and tree boughs that they cut, carry and weave into a structure of considerable strength. The dam's purpose is to slow the flow of a small stream until the water depth surrounding the lodge allows sufficient protection from predators. The lodge's only entrance is under the water. Additionally, the dam creates important wetlands that serve as a habitat to many types of waterfowl, amphibians, fish and numerous other animals, water and plant life.

In the seventeenth century, both Native American and European trappers captured and traded beaver pelts (skins). The beaver pelts were in great demand for making fashionable beaver fur hats and for trim on coats. The Adirondacks' abundant beaver population was a major reason for the French, Dutch and English establishing trading posts in New York State. The over-trapping caused the beavers' extirpation in the Adirondacks. Years

This abandoned beaver lodge must have been built too close to the road, threatening to flood the area. It is likely that DEC trapped the beavers and relocated them to a more secluded region.

later, the Department of Environmental Conversation imported beaver families, reintroducing them to the Adirondacks. Beavers are now protected through regulated trapping.

SPOTLIGHT ON: BELOW ZERO

Zero degrees (actually fifty-two degrees below zero, a temperature recorded on February 9, 1934), is an example of some of the low temperatures that have been recorded in the Adirondacks.

Regional Adirondack temperature data shows some thirty-five to forty-five days a year with below-zero temperatures. The region's average annual mean temperature is forty degrees, with an average mean January temperature of sixteen degrees. Even in the summer months of June and August, it is not uncommon for night temperatures to approach the freezing levels. The northern areas of the Adirondack Park have a seasonal average snowfall in excess of 90 inches, while Tug Hill can expect a seasonal snowfall of about 175 inches. Lakes can freeze with ice depths of up to 36 inches deep.

Swings in temperatures are considered a normal part of Adirondack weather. In the summer of 1816, severe temperature swings occurred, resulting in devastating cold spells. Food shortages ensued and eventually became the basis for a number of Adirondack residents leaving the area for milder weather and richer soils. Adirondack

Opposite: An Adirondack snow-covered stream in March shows signs of spring thaw as its center starts to become visible.

Alfred Hayes stands atop a sizeable snowbank. The car below looks like a child's toy. Photo taken near Salisbury, New York.

farmers at that time were subsistence farmers growing food for their own survival and that of their livestock needs. The remoteness of the Adirondacks made it nearly impossible to quickly transport daily staples from unaffected neighboring districts.

In 1816, from May through September, long cold snaps killed vegetable plants and fruit tree blossoms and stunted pasture growth for feeding livestock. Some mornings during these summer months, Adirondackers awoke to find quarter-inch-thick ice on lakes, a heavy frost covering the fields or a blanket of snow coating the pastures. Not every day was wintry. Temperatures often would swing back to normal summer readings of eighty to ninety degrees, but without warning, an uncommon two- or three-day cold snap would follow.

The 1816 "Year Without a Summer," also known as "Eighteen Hundred and Froze to Death," was contributed to the volcanic eruption the previous year on Mount Tambora near Java. This powerful eruption cast into the atmosphere volcanic dust, providing a sunscreen that caused a cooling of the earth's atmosphere, especially in the northeastern United States.

Fun Activity!
Animal Tracks in the Adirondacks

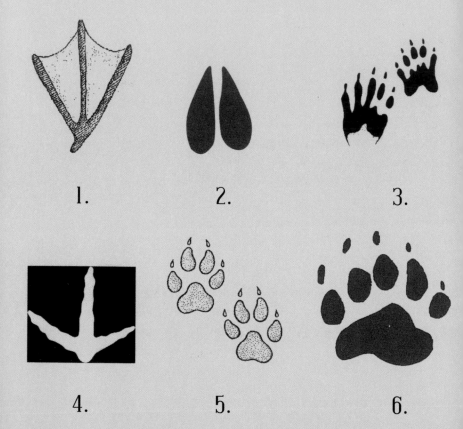

1.

2.

3.

4.

5.

6.

Identify the Animal to Its Tracks

1.

2.

3.

4.

5.

6.

Once the worksheet is complete, take it outdoors near a lake or stream or even a large mud puddle. At a water source, you should find animal tracks.

See if any of the tracks near the water source match any animal tracks on your worksheet. Which new tracks have you discovered? Which classification of animals have you found the most tracks of: mammal, fowl or amphibian?

Chapter 3

People of the Adirondacks

The first to seek out the Adirondacks were from the surrounding valleys. The French explorers built trading posts along major waterways like the Mohawk Valley, Lake George and Lake Champlain for profitable fur trade. Indians used the woods as their summer hunting grounds. Later came the logging and mining industries. The area was known to be unsuitable for agriculture. In the 1700s, Lewis Evans wrote his opinion of the regions as a "drowned impassable land."

The hardy stock of individuals who did stay found some means to endure the hardships. Survival in the Adirondacks carries with it a certain dignity of having a rugged quality. Even those city vacationers who stay for a short couple of weeks take back with them particular woodsman bragging rights.

Adirondack residents were folks who had to be resourceful to survive not only the isolation but also the brutal winters

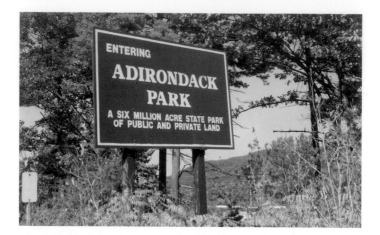

"Entering Adirondack Park" sign near Exit 21, Lake George, on the Adirondack Northway. The Northway was put through the Adirondacks in the 1950s, one of the few exceptions allowed by the Adirondack Park Agency. At most Adirondack Park entry points, there are similar welcoming signs.

and economic uncertainty. A few with certain personality and character forever left their marks on history. Their acts influenced on a larger scale and were known through the United States and even abroad. From capitalist hotelier Apollos Paul Smith, to social reformer John Brown, to affluent architectural designer W.W. Durant, to environmental advocate Verplanck Colvin, all came from different paths of life and left equally varied impacts on the Adirondack Park.

Spotlight On: John Brown

John Brown, an abolitionist, farmer, tanner and surveyor, was born in May 1800 in Torrington, Connecticut. He moved his family to the Lake Placid area in 1849 to oversee Gerrit Smith's experimental free black settlement, later named Timbuktu. Brown's task was to help these freed African Americans become self-sustaining farmers. Smith gave to freed black men forty acres to cultivate and become prosperous farmers in an attempt to meet the newly reinstated New York State land voting requirements. In helping Smith, Brown developed a growing interest in the abolitionist movement. This ultimately pulled him away from his North Elba family for extended periods while he pursued antislavery campaigns in states like Kansas, which eventually became a free state. What John Brown is most famous for is his participation in the raid on Harpers Ferry. This assault's intentions were to capture the U.S. Arsenal at Harpers Ferry then use the arms in the continued campaign to liberate slaves in the South by giving arms to slaves. Brown was captured two days after the raid, imprisoned, tried for treason and later hanged in Charlestown, Virginia, on December 2, 1859. His body was sent back to North Elba, where it was buried on his farm on December 8. Seeking equality for all men, black and white, John Brown paid the highest price in his unceasing antislavery endeavor.

A statue of abolitionist John Brown with his arm around the shoulders of a young African American boy. With the intentions to arm a slave revolt, Brown directed the raid on Harpers Ferry in 1859.

Spotlight On: Verplanck Colvin

Verplanck Colvin (1847–1920) grew up in Albany, New York. He became a key individual, leading the cry for New York State to create the Adirondack Park with its preservation as "forever wild" status.

In his youth, Colvin grew up exploring Albany County's surrounding woods and fields and had an unquenchable fascination for wilderness discovery. After high school, he joined his father's law firm, where his interest in topography offered him opportunities to settle landownership and boundary disputes. Yet Colvin longed to be out adventuring the natural world. In 1872, he convinced the New York State legislature to employ him in mapping the first New York State Land Survey. These surveys located, measured and mapped a bird's-eye view of the Adirondack region's physical geography. This task lasted for twenty-eight years, and in that time, Colvin and his crew measured the heights of mountains and the depths of lakes, collected and recorded weather and temperatures, documented animal and plant life and pencil sketched reality in the Adirondacks.

Prior maps of the Adirondacks were crude and inaccurate, often showing misdirected river flows. The Adirondack Survey located numerous undocumented lakes, streams and mountains, many of which were not known to exist prior to the New York State survey.

Early survey measurements employed several methods, including the use of the compass, barometer, vertical measuring rods and the theodolite. The barometer uses air pressure as an indication of height. The vertical measuring rod is a kind of a ruler, a steel rod of known distance, used as a reference in making a measurement. The theodolite is a telescope that sets on a tripod and measures both horizontal and vertical angles. The theodolite is used in combination with a technique called triangulation. Verplanck Colvin started his survey of the Adirondacks using the triangulation method. Using precisely known heights and distance benchmarks (Crown Point's lighthouse and Barber's Point lighthouse), the surveyors could then apply mathematical calculations to determine the height and distance of the unknown mountain to be measured. Their first measurement was Mount Summit. This procedure was then applied to other unknown elevations and distances throughout the Adirondacks, charting the peaks' actual positions, distances and elevations.

To accurately view some of the mountain summits, Colvin designed the Stan-Helio. This reflective device, positioned on top of a large log pyramid tower, aided in measuring mountain distances. This device was made of wired sheets of new tin set out at various angles to reflect the sunlight and could be easily seen with the naked eye from twenty-five miles away or from fifty miles using a telescope.

While mapping the Adirondacks, Colvin saw the devastation on the area's terrain brought on by clear-cut lumbering. He pressed the need to preserve New York's forests, halt erosion and secure future water supplies. He realized that the Adirondacks contain the springs that are the source of principal headwaters of New York's chief rivers. He believed that current lumbering practices could threaten the viability of the Erie Canal: "Unless the regions be preserved essentially in its present wilderness conditions the ruthless burning and destruction of the forest will slowly, year after year, creep onward…and vast areas of naked rock, arid sand, and gravel will alone remain to receive the bounty of the clouds and be unable to retain it."

SPOTLIGHT ON: WILLIAM WEST DURANT

William West Durant, son of the wealthy surgeon-turned-railroad-tycoon Dr. Thomas Clark Durant, was largely responsible for opening the Adirondacks to tourists. W.W. Durant, wanting the woodland beauties to be accessible to the world, began to set in place accommodation of transportation and recreation unheard of in this area. Durant brought railroads, coaches and steamboats to navigate the difficulties of the Adirondack landscape. In 1871, he completed the Adirondack Railroad, which ran some sixty miles from Saratoga to North Creek. He further established accessibility to Blue Mountain Lake and on to Raquette Lake. To this area he brought Concord coaches that ran from North Creek to

Blue Mountain Lake, a distance of thirty miles. He brought steamboats, capable of handling two hundred passengers, to carry people from Blue Mountain to Raquette. He set in place telegraph lines, churches and golf courses. With all these modern-day comforts and amenities, tourism increased, and W.W. Durant became known fondly as a distinguished woodland host.

What Durant was most noted for was his creative, artistic architectural design that became known as "Great Camps." His unique style assembled elements of Swiss chalets and arts and crafts–era influences while using Adirondack rustic materials: enormous log beams, local fieldstone

Above: W.W. Durant's Great Camp Sagamore was a unique architectural design influenced by Swiss chalets, constructed using natural Adirondack resources as building materials.

Opposite: Durant used natural materials in his Great Camp design. This photo exemplifies his style in this side porch shot of Camp Sagamore.

fireplaces, taxidermy animals, white birch bark and spruce twigs. The combination of decorative style has become an Adirondack icon. Durant's first camp building venture was Camp Pine Knot located on Raquette Lake. The camps became a series of clustered buildings. The separation of each structure's purpose was to prevent fire from wiping out all the dwellings while creating a sense of privacy in a small settlement atmosphere.

SPOTLIGHT ON: PAUL SMITH

Early in his youth, **Paul Smith** caught an industrial spirit being around his father's many Vermont businesses, including sawmills, gristmills and logging operations. His home located near Lake Champlain allowed ten-year-old Paul employment opportunities with the lake's shipping and transportation commerce. At this time, Lake Champlain was bustling, as merchant canalboats shipped south to New York City lumber, grain, coal, iron ore, hay, stone, apples, butter, cheese, flax, potatoes, cattle, sheep and hogs. Return trips north mostly brought back goods from Europe, including salt, tea, cloth and New York City vacationers.

Smith initially worked as a canalboat operator, eventually building and running his own canalboat. In this occupation, he met many well-known, wealthy and politically connected men who took a liking to Smith, inviting him to join them for some Adirondack outdoor excursions. Smith's familiarity with the woods made him perfectly suited to guide their expeditions, uncovering idyllic settings for fishing, hunting and camping.

Smith had a constant drive for business endeavors, and seeing an opportunity to house and guide adventurous men of wealth, he made plans to open his own remote wilderness retreat. Purchasing two hundred acres for one dollar per acre, in 1853 he opened Hunter House, a small rustic inn with eight to ten bedrooms along

Lake George has always been a big tourism town. A must when visiting the village is the steamboat ride. Here, one returns from a late afternoon excursion.

the Saranac River. Hunter House was a huge success. The meals were outstanding, featuring hunter's fare of venison, lake trout, partridge and turkey, along with country staples such as chicken, ham and beef. Smith, an excellent guide and most likeable personality, spun humorous tales of Adirondack adventures, all adding to the inn's appeal.

In the fall of 1858, Smith and his Boston lawyer friend, Daniel Saunders, were exploring the southwest/ northeast side of St. Regis Lake. Both men found this site particularly serene. Saunders encouraged Smith to open a larger lodge with all the modern-day comforts

Smith's Hotel, one of the first wilderness resorts in the Adirondacks, located on the shores of Saint Regis Lake. The hotel burned in 1937

and now is the site of Paul Smith's College. *Courtesy of the Library of Congress.*

to accommodate families. The following summer, Smith and his wife, Lydia, opened Paul Smith's Hotel on that very spot. Like Hunter House, this new hotel became a beloved Adirondack summer retreat hugely popular in the United States and abroad. Guests returned year after year. They told friends and brought extended family there to vacation.

Smith's ambitious spirit kept him constantly improving the hotel. He ran stagecoaches to pick up his guests from the nearest train station some forty miles away. Eventually, he built and ran Paul Smith's Electric Railroad from Lake Clear to his hotel. He expanded the hotel from 17 to 250 rooms, able to accommodate five hundred guests. He added a casino, bowling alley, poolroom, dance hall, golf course and baseball field. He opened a general store so local residents, along with hotel guests, could purchase camping supplies, food and other essentials. Other businesses he started were Paul Smith's Telegraph Co., Paul Smith's Telephone Co. and Paul Smith's Electric Light and Power Co.

With a genuine capitalist spirit, the Paul Smith empire started as a small, rustic hunting camp and eventually became a world-famous summer family resort. Notable people such as Theodore Roosevelt, Calvin Coolidge and P.T. Barnum were guests. Over the years, Smith acquired thirty thousand acres including some ten lakes. In December 1912, Paul Smith died at the age of eighty-seven, leaving behind the hotel businesses to his two remaining sons. Smith had devoted his life to its creation. In 1937, the hotel caught fire. Today on the site is Paul Smith's College, offering two- and four-year degrees in culinary, hotel and restaurant hospitality; biology and environmental studies; liberal arts; and business studies.

Fun Activity!

Building a Wooden Adirondack Lean-to

Supplies List: Vertical supports (two), horizontal support (one), roof rafters (approximately ten), garden string or small grapevines, side supports (eight), several pine bows, leaves and a pocketknife.

1. Choose a site for building. Consider an area with flat ground and some additional trees for cover that faces south. The site should also be an area where flooding won't occur.
2. Locate/find construction material to build the support. (a) Vertical supports—approximately four to five feet above ground. This can be two trees five to six feet apart or fence posts or two sturdy five-foot branches. If you use sturdy branches, you must dig a hole into the ground one foot deep and bury one end of each branch into the ground. (b) Horizontal support—find a six-foot sturdy branch and then, using grapevines or garden string, attach the horizontal branch to the two vertical supports. At this point, your structure will look similar to football goal posts.
3. Roof frame. The remaining longer gathered branches are placed one end on the horizontal support while the other end rests on the ground. Depending on the width of your lean-to, there should be at least ten roof frame branches. These roof frame branches can be fastened to the horizontal support with twine or small grapevine branches.
4. Roofing material. Gather a collection of pine tree bows, overlapping leaf branches, leaves, tree bark slabs, lumber planks or a tarp or poncho. If using branches or leaves,

Children at camp, Raquette Lake, Adirondack Mountains, New York. An open, three sided lean-to made of nearby logs can be seen, along with the rock-encircled fire pit in front used for warmth and cooking. *Courtesy of the Library of Congress.*

a covering of intersecting layers is most effective in keeping out the elements. Tie down as needed.

5. Side Protection. On each side of the lean-to support, place various lengths of smaller branches to provide side protection. This will minimize wind draft. Add pine tree bows, tree bark slabs or leaf branches to the side supports. Tie down as needed.

6. Flooring. Again, pine tree bows, leaves or small leaf branches provide a nice flooring. Gather enough to be off the damp ground.

7. Grab your sleeping bag and enjoy.

Tip: Use strongest branches for construction of the frame, horizontal and vertical supports.

Chapter 4

Working in the
Adirondacks

David Henderson, owner of the Tahawus Mine, once said of the surrounding forest, "If the land in that wilderness is to have any value at all it will only be in consequence of our operation at the Adirondack Works." This early mindset of the taking of natural resources to the point of elimination was done with one goal: to squeeze the most profit from the land. It was done in all types of Adirondack industry, including but not limited to mining, logging and pulp and charcoal making. Additionally, it was a common practice that once the land was purchased inexpensively and all profits had been reaped, the property would be abandoned to go back for taxes. This practice alone represented Adirondack industries' common practice and ideology: if a dollar wasn't to be harvested from the North Woods, it was of no value to them. While their history cast many great stories of capitalist spirit, some of those industries' repeated devastation on the environment left landscape scars for years. The take and desert ideology formed the underpinnings as to why conservationists pushed for Adirondack Park protection from future pillage in the Adirondack State Park. Radical action was needed to protect the North Woods, and voters of New York State amended our state constitution to make the forest "forever wild." Today, some argue that we need to loosen these restrictions to help the small Adirondack hamlets from becoming ghost towns.

Above: This lightweight pontoon plane prepares for takeoff from Sacandaga Lake, Speculator, New York.

Opposite: Fishing has always been a favorite activity in the Adirondacks. The region's miles of streams and numerous ponds and lakes provide ample opportunity for any angler. The state fish of New York is the speckled trout.

Spotlight On: Lumber

Lumber from the Adirondacks was in great demand following the Revolutionary War as the state sought a way to pay off its war debts. The pine trees, some 150 feet tall with a diameter of 6 feet across, were cut and sold to France and England for their shipbuilding. These first large timbers were used for the tall masts of large ships. The next big solicitation for the trees in the Adirondacks came from the demands of an expanding nation. A flourishing New York State found uses for the timber in

Above: Logs on Lake Flower by S. Merchant's Lumber. The Adirondack streams were the most cost-effective transportation available in such a rugged Adirondack terrain. *Courtesy of the Adirondack Room, Saranac Lake Free Library, Copy and Reuse Restrictions Apply.*

Opposite: The lumber industry used horses to haul the logs on bobsleds to the landing. *Courtesy of the Adirondack Room, Saranac Lake Free Library, Copy and Reuse Restrictions Apply.*

constructing city structures, the laying of railroads and building people's homes. Other uses were in flooring and the construction of pianos, billiard tables and furniture. Later, with the invention of pulp-grinding machines, nearly every tree in the woods would be taken, clear-cutting even the smallest trees for pulp used in the making of paper products.

The lumbering industry had a season for different aspects of the lumbering process. The cutting or felling of the trees occurred during the months of May through August. It was at this time that loggers would peel the bark by using a tool called a spud. These trees would lie on the ground until winter, the start of the official skidding season. When winter arrived, the logs would be loaded onto the sleds. Teams of horses would then pull the loads of logs to the landing along the river. A large wooden water box mounted on a sled was used to sprinkle water on skid way roads, sometimes ten miles long, making

them smooth and easier to glide the sled of logs. The logs would be piled at the river's edge or usually on the frozen water, waiting for the spring thaw. In spring, when the ice broke, the logs were tossed into the water, floating the river rapids to a mill downstream. This process became known as log driving, sending logs down a narrow, rocky, swift-flowing stream to the mill. Using the nearby streams as a navigable log highway made cutting lumber in otherwise inaccessible, impenetrable areas possible as well as lucrative. Some of these trees were in areas where roads or railroads could not be built due to the rugged terrain, steep mountains or wet marshes.

Laws were passed in New York to allow the lumber companies to log drive, where the river was used as a "public highway." Many lumber companies built dams to hold back the river's water until the time of the drive. They would open the dam, releasing thousands of gallons of water so the logs would float downstream in the rapid currents. They would lift the splash boards holding back the water, letting the water out of the spillway and sending the logs down the creek, some traveling as far as forty miles downstream; this was called "tripping the dam." At the end of the day, the splashboards would be put back in so water would accumulate overnight for the next day's drive.

Spotlight On: Mining

Mining the Adirondacks occurred in many sections of the park, employed a sizeable workforce, lasted over an extended period of time and extracted a variety of minerals, including iron ore, titanium, marble, graphite, lead, talc, granite, limestone and sandstone. Mining the Adirondack Park region's minerals contributed significantly to the United States' industrial expansion. This region's mineral deposits become crucial to U.S. national security during World War II. In the 1800s, as many as two hundred mines were in operation.

Besides a seemingly inexhaustible mineral supply, mining success in this region relied on an abundant nearby supply of wood from the North Woods forest. The nearby forest was the means that made the charcoal that fueled the mines' blast furnaces. The mining industry additionally relied on constructed dammed water power to run the equipment of the mines, such as the bellows that stimulated the blast of air to the forge's fire. Equally important was the accessibility to a railroad or a navigable waterway, as the rugged terrain of the Adirondacks made the building and maintaining of roads an unfavorable transportation alternative.

The mine provided employment opportunities for local Adirondacks residents, boosting the local community from nothing to a thriving community with schools, banks, recreation fields, hospitals, sawmills and blacksmith shops. The mine's initial workforce consisted of immigrant labor.

Nelson Rockefeller made the Barton garnet the New York State official gemstone.

The immigrants eventually stayed and became third- and fourth-generation miners. Its workers were seen as rugged, independent people with strong loyalties to the mines that employed them.

From the heart of the Adirondack crust were extracted numerous minerals used then and now for a variety of purposes:

Iron ore was initially used in the Revolutionary War to outfit naval vessels. The pig iron, which is a term used to define iron that is shipped for later remanufacturing, eventually was used to make cannons, grates and cast-iron stoves. The steel cables in the Brooklyn Bridge and George Washington Bridge were manufactured using the iron extracted from Adirondack iron ore deposits.

Titanium, used as a whitening agent for paints, was of huge importance in World War II as the United States' supplies were cut off. Titanium was also used to make smoke screens, another World War II weapon.

Talc is used for ceramics.

Red garnet, now New York State's official gem, was used in making abrasives for sandpaper.

Wollastonite's uses were discovered after World War II in ceramics, paints, plastics and building materials. This material makes products durable due to its needle-like particles.

Graphite is used for black pencil lead.

Sandstone is used extensively to construct public buildings. It is especially popular in church construction and is also good for making sandpaper.

Limestone is used in construction and to neutralize acidic soils.

Marble in any limestone that will take a polish is used in construction in addition to monuments. Many of Cornell University's foundations came from the Adirondack mines.

Lead was used to make musket balls.

SPOTLIGHT ON: RAILROADS

Railroads in the Adirondacks consisted of a handful of short, unconnected, randomly scattered rail lines compared to other U.S. tracks. In 1869, the Union Pacific and Central Railroads together laid over 1,700 miles of continuous tracks in our country's first Transcontinental Railroad, connecting California to Iowa. The Adirondack tracks, however, were shorter in distance and not continuous, having many small spurs branching from the main line. The Chateaugay Railroad from Plattsburgh to Lake Placid, for example, was only 83 miles long. The shorter Adirondack Railroad tributaries were constructed to penetrate the wilderness interior in an effort to extract the abundant natural resources. During the late 1800s, the United States needed the untapped Adirondack resources to accommodate a growing country. Freight trains made available natural resources from Adirondack pulp mills, sawmills, charcoal kilns, iron mines, tanneries and stone and gravel quarries. Additionally, Adirondack passenger trains deposited into the wilderness summer tourists, tuberculosis patients, wealthy camp owners, mail, Dannemora prisoners and prison supplies.

During its construction, the railroad employed workers to cut the path, emplace retaining walls, build bridges and trusses and lay ties and tracks. In addition to employing many Adirondack people, the railroad gave Adirondack artisans a vessel to ship their goods to market. Locally made goods

The northernmost stop, the North Creek Railroad Train Station, built in 1872, received wealthy Gilded Age vacationers. It has been restored to the original structure. On September 14, 1901, Theodore Roosevelt learned of his succession to then President McKinley at this station.

like milk, cheese, butter, furniture, wagons, carriages and ice blocks all had a market in the city just a train ride away.

The 1930s saw the start of the demise of the Adirondack Railroad usage for both passenger travel and freight transportation. Railroads were being replaced by paved roads for automobiles, trucks and buses, all new modes of Adirondack transportation.

Other factors contributing to the Adirondack Railroad demise were forest depletion and the introduction of refrigeration. Ice blocks were cut, stored and shipped to the cities from the numerous northern lakes. At the same time, many milk stations closed, as now trucks would pick up the cans of milk from each farm. Soon it became unprofitable to run the trains, pay workers and maintain the tracks. The usefulness of the Adirondack Railroad came full circle. In the 1940s, these railroads gave once more of themselves as several tracks were salvaged for their steel in the war effort. The daily whistles echoing down the riverbed or over the mountain grew silent as the Adirondacks' railroads were permanently dismissed, left to become wilderness again.

SPOTLIGHT ON: KILNS

Kilns for the making of charcoal became common on the Adirondack landscape from the mid-1800s to the early 1900s. The charcoal kilns are dome shaped and made of brick and stone, allowing the carefully stacked wood inside to burn slowly by controlling the amount of oxygen to the burn. The burn would take anywhere from three to ten days. One cord of wood would yield, on average, thirty-five to forty bushels of charcoal.

Charcoal was needed in large quantities to fuel the blast furnaces for the mining and iron operations in the production of pig iron. Charcoal was considered superior over wood, as it burned hotter and cleaner. Charcoal is made from hardwoods that have been burned in an oxygen-deficient environment. Charcoal makers, called colliers, made charcoal from hardwood trees, preferring

Kilns are dome-shaped brick structures used to make charcoal. Wood was stacked in a means for a slow burn. Charcoal was the preferred fuel of mining operations. *Courtesy of the Adirondack Room, Saranac Lake Free Library, Copy and Reuse Restrictions Apply.*

to use beech, birch and maple. Eventually, every tree close to the kilns was cut and used. Charcoal makers were the first to use the practice of clear-cutting a forest. To make one ton of iron required as much as five hundred bushels of charcoal. During this time, Chateaugay Ore and Iron Company cut two thousand acres a year to feed its seventy kilns. David Henderson, owner of the Tahawus Mine, articulated his view of the Adirondack land: "If land in that wilderness is to have any value at all, it will only be in consequences of our operation at the Adirondack Works."

Spotlight On: Potash and Pearlash

Potash and **pearlash** are wood byproducts used in the late 1700s and 1800s in the making of soap, glass and coloring fabrics. As implied by their names, potash and pearlash are substances left from the ashes of hardwood trees. These two products provided early Adirondack settlers with a much-needed cash crop. Potash and its further refined pearlash became highly valued commodities used at home and sold as an article of trade in the United States as well as exported directly to England.

The first Adirondack settlers were faced with the challenges of opening up the dense forest to fields suitable for planting crops. This required the tiring task of felling trees, cutting the logs for lumber or firewood and finally removing the stumps, along with the deeply embedded roots. The easiest way to dispose of the excess wood (roots, stumps and small limbs) was to burn them as they lay.

When a fair amount of wood ashes had been collected from the stump burnings, settlers would place the ashes in a lye-leaching barrel. This bottomless barrel sat on a grooved stone. At the bottom of the barrel was first placed a layer of straw, followed by a layer of small twigs. The ashes would be placed on top, water would be poured over the ashes and the lye would filter through the layers of twigs and straw and finally leak into a collection pail from the groove in the stone. The collected lye liquid would be boiled until the solution would be able to float an egg, a measurement used to determine good-quality potash. Pearlash required further processing of baking the potash liquid solution until it became white in color.

Soap making was one of the first uses of potash. Soap was made by combining the boiling wood ash lye (potash) with rendered animal fats. The mixture of grease and potash was boiled until soap was formed, taking six to eight hours. By adding common table salts to the mixture, the soap would harden; without the salt additive, the soap would be jelly-like. Having plenty of both of these items, early colonists used their creativity and self-supporting nature by making soap.

SPOTLIGHT ON: UPPER WORKS

Upper Works, Tahawus, McIntyre Mine or Adirondack Iron Works are all names given to the location of the iron ore claim between Lake Sanford and Lake Henderson near the beginning of the Hudson River. The original visible iron ore discovery was fifty feet wide, and the surrounding iron ore deposits were believed to be so large that they were of national importance.

The old McIntyre blast furnace is now under restoration efforts. This enormous stone structure worked much like a blacksmith fire, where large bellows forced air to increase the fire's temperature.

Abenaki Indian Lewis Elijah presented a small prospecting party initially in the area looking for silver deposits with a rather large bar of iron ore. For $1.50 and some tobacco, Lewis showed the prospectors—Duncan McMartin, David Henderson and John McIntyre—to the vein of ore. Upon seeing their discovery, the group immediately set out to Albany to file their claim. They eventually purchased over 100,000 acres around the discovery site.

Within a year of discovery, members of the search party, headed by Archibald McIntyre, built a forge and housing for the workers. Horses and wagons took the mined ore to Lake Champlain over crude mountain roads. This process was both laborious and time consuming. From Lake Champlain, the ore was sent by barge to Jersey City, New Jersey, and other mills.

THE MINE AT WORK

- Capacity of fourteen tons of iron per day
- Employed four hundred workers
- Sixty-foot-tall blast furnace whose fuel supply, charcoal, was made from local supply of trees
- A large amount of water power needed to power the bellows
- In order to make the mine profitable, needed a railroad
- Wilderness becomes a village: five houses, store, blacksmith shop, carpenter shop, bank, coal house and two barns
- 1850–51, London's World Fair, McIntyre Mine's iron ore won an award for its high-quality American steel

DIFFICULTIES/OBSTACLES FOR MINE MAKING MONEY AND EXPANDING

- No railroad, which was needed to make the mine profitable
- Competition with other mines opening in the United States and other countries
- Seemed to be an impurity in the ore called titanium, which ruined its reputation as a good-quality ore for making iron, meeting newly established steel specification

During the Upper Works' most productive iron ore years, Archibald's son-in-law, David Henderson, a member of the original prospecting party, supervised the mine. In September 1845, while looking in the area for a larger body of water power, Henderson died from an accidental gunshot wound from his own pistol at a spot later named Calamity Pond.

As they were unable to make a profit, iron ore operations ceased in 1857. The following year, Archibald McIntyre died. From the late 1800s to 1940, the mine lands and structures were leased to various sporting clubs for recreational use only. It wasn't until eighty-three years after its closing that the mined was reopened. With the outbreak of World War II, the United States' supply of titanium from India was cut off. Titanium dioxide, an element needed in making white paints and enamels for painting U.S. military tanks, planes and other war vehicles, was in demand. Knowing the McIntyre Mine to be the largest source of titanium in this county, in 1941, National Lead (NL) Company purchased McIntyre Iron Company's assets, reviving the mine, employing 325 people and eventually shipping two thousand tons of titanium dioxide a day. In 1943, with the help of the government, twenty-nine miles of railroad was laid, finally connecting the mine to North Creek. In 1982, NL Company closed the mine.

Today, the trail leading to the Upper Works site is a popular hiking destination. The Open Space Institute (OSI) purchased the Upper Works, including some 9,646 acres, from NL Company for $8.5 million in 2003. OSI secured the land "to protect scenic, natural, and historic landscapes to ensure public enjoyment, conserve habitats, and sustain community character." OSI set out to preserve four historically significant mine structures: the blast furnace; the Mount Adams fire tower; the Upper Preston Pond hunting camp; and MacNaughton Cottage, the camp where then vice president Teddy Roosevelt stayed for a hiking and camping outing. While staying there, he received news that President McKinley had been assassinated.

In March 2008, New York State purchased from OSI 6,813 acres of the Upper Works property for $5.96 million, adding to the Adirondack Forest Preserve and protecting numerous mountains, lakes and streams for public enjoyment for years to come.

Fun Activity!

Soap Making–An Adirondack Commodity

1 Pound Cold-Process Soap Making

Materials for Safety: Protective safety goggles, gloves (examination/nursing or well-fitted kitchen rubber gloves), long-sleeve shirt, bottle of vinegar to pour on any lye spills if they occur. <u>Note: Prepare lye and water solution in a well-ventilated area.</u>

Two four-cup glass measuring cups to mix lye solution, heat the oils and blend the soap. One for the lye mixture, second for the oil mixture.

Stainless steel spoons, candy thermometer, soap mold (baby wipe container or small shoe box lined with garbage bag), immersion blender (shortens the stirring time)

Ingredients
Lye Solution
Lye, 2.4 ounces
Water, 6 ounces
Oils
Olive oil, 10.5 ounces
Coconut oil, 5.25 ounces
Castor oil, 1 tablespoon
Additives
1 tablespoon of essential oils <u>or</u>
1 teaspoon of fragrance oil like lily of the valley or jasmine

Instructions (to be done with an adult)

1. Put on safety goggles, gloves and long-sleeve shirt.
2. In a well-ventilated area, carefully add 2.4 ounces of lye to 6 ounces of water. Stir well; do not breathe the fumes. Set aside to cool to 110 degrees.
3. Add the oils together in the second heat-proof glass four-cup measuring container and melt them down over boiling water (like a double boiler). Allow them to cool to approximately 110 degrees.
4. When both mixtures are at 110 degrees, slowly pour the lye solution into the oils, stir until trace occurs a thin, pudding consistency. The immersion blender will quicken the process; otherwise, it will take an hour by hand.
5. When the soap mixture traces, pour into the prepared mold.
6. Cover the mold with plastic wrap and then wrap the mold in a towel for two days.
7. After two to three days, turn over your mold and gently push the bottom to loosen the soap from the mold. Put it in the freezer for an hour and then try to remove.
8. Use a stainless steel knife to cut soap into bars and put into a brown paper bag to dry, turning every day.
9. In four weeks, soap will be ready to use. Enjoy!

Chapter 5

Places, Events and Organizations

O ur world is one where natural resources are limited, some finite. Once contaminated, damaged, disfigured or totally eliminated, their restoration can be impossible. During the first part of the nineteenth century, unchecked capitalist self-interest plundered the Adirondack forest through means of logging and mining operations. Trees disappeared by the millions and open-pit mining blemished surrounding mountains, while trophy hunters wiped out entire Adirondack native species, including moose, mountain lion, beaver and deer.

By the mid-nineteenth century, having seen the Adirondack landscape so injured, residents began to express concerns about the need to shield the forest from the present pillage. It was their concern that the Adirondacks were needed to guarantee New York City and New York State their source of an adequate water supply. For several years to follow, New York State voters took action by passing laws

These early 1900s hikers look east from Bald Mountain trail.
Courtesy of the Library of Congress.

to protect the Adirondacks from future environmental ruin. To gain an appreciation for the arduous legislative steps New York State endured to defend the Adirondack State Park, below are listed key amendments and actions taken to get that protection:

1874: Verplanck Colvin, while supervising the survey of the Adirondack wilderness, observed the unchecked destruction of the forest. In his reports to the legislature, he called for the creation of an Adirondack Forest Preserve.

1885: New York State legislation established the Forest Preserve in eleven Adirondack counties to be kept as wild forest lands. The Forest Preserve is that section of New York State's Adirondacks owned in common by the people of the state of New York. (Logging restrictions not mentioned.)

1892: 2.8-million-acre Adirondack Park established by the state, consisting of 681,000 acres of Forest Preserve. The blue line was established as an area where the state was to concentrate on purchasing private lands. (Logging still continues.)

1894: Constitutional convention committee drafts an amendment barring the lease, sale or exchange of lands and prohibits the sale, removal or destruction of timber.

1894: Constitutional protection, Article XIV of the New York State Constitution, the Forest Preserve lands are under the highest level of protection: "forever wild." This law became effective on January 1, 1895.

1968: Governor Rockefeller assigned a study commission. This commission recommended the creation of the Adirondack Park Agency (APA), having the powers to oversee the use and development of public and private lands in the blue line.

1970: Department of Conservation (DEC) responsible for managing parkland in compliance with the APA guidelines, also in charge of new land acquisition. Duties are to conserve, improve and protect the natural resources.

1971: Adirondack Park Agency created, responsible for developing and maintaining land-use plans on both private and public lands within the Adirondack Park blue line.

SPOTLIGHT ON: DEPARTMENT OF ENVIRONMENTAL CONSERVATION (DEC)

Early accounts of Adirondack history show that people felt they could conquer and exploit nature for a quick profit. This is evident in the devastating clear-cutting of the Adirondack forest to meet a growing nation's thirst for lumber used in the construction of buildings, railroads, pulp for paper and the making of charcoal used in the mining industry. Following this period, people's attitudes began to change toward nurturing and preserving New York State's environment. This awareness led to the creation of the **Department of Environmental Conservation** (DEC) on July 1, 1970. Its mission is to "conserve, improve, and protect its natural resources and environment, and control water, land, and air pollution, in order to enhance the health, safety and welfare of the people of the state and their overall economic and social well being."

As its goal to promote public recreation and safety, the DEC:

Promotes Public Recreation and Safety

- Maintains forty-four Adirondack campsites, along with boat launches, so visitors can camp, swim, hike, fish and explore outdoor activities in the Adirondacks.
- Publishes the *New York State Conservationist*, a bimonthly magazine covering topics on New York's communities, wildlife and environment.

Bogs have highly acidic water, as they have no supply of fresh water other than rainfall.

Along trails, you will see the signs marking "Forest Preserve." These are the lands are owned by the people of the State of New York.

- Issues fishing, hunting and trapping licenses and provides hunter safety courses.
- Operates year-round education interpretive centers for environmental awareness at Five Rivers EEC, Stony Kill Farm EEC, Rogers EEC and Reinstein Nature Preserve, as well as DEC summer camps for kids twelve to seventeen years old.

Protects Environmental Quality
- Educates and enforces laws to clean up the environment: air pollution, water pollution and recycling.

Protects New York State Natural Resources
- Ensures abundant populations of fish and wildlife; clean lakes and rivers; and rich, thriving forest growth.
- Monitors mining.
- Manages state forest, including programs like planting trees.

- Purchases lands for public use. New York State has preserved millions of acres by buying lands previously owed by individuals for future recreation: 144,000 acres of land formerly owned by Champion International Co.; 14,700 acres of Whitney Park in Hamilton County; and 10,000 acres from NL Company, formerly the Tahawus Tract, a titanium and iron mine in Essex County.
- Manages deer population through recreational hunting.
- Operates the Salmon River Fish Hatchery in Oswego County to raise salmon and trout for stocking local lakes and streams.
- Protects rare plants and animals in danger of extinction by reestablishing animals like the bald eagle, beaver and turkey in parts of the state where they no longer exist.

SPOTLIGHT ON: FIRE TOWERS

Fire towers, once fifty-seven in number, could be found on mountain peaks in the Adirondacks. The height of these steel towers ranged from forty to seventy feet. Men called rangers or observers, whose job it was to closely survey the area for forest fires, occupied the fire towers.

On top of the towers, a small window-encased shelter afforded the ranger a 360-degree view of the surrounding mountains. The observer's tools usually consisted of a compass, field glasses, topographical maps of the surrounding area and a telephone connection to the fire warden. Using these tools, the ranger could accurately

The great fires of 1903 and 1908 devoured one million acres of forest.
Adirondack citizens grew concerned about forest fire management.

discover and locate a fire's source some thirty miles away. Some of the best observers could tell from the color of the smoke the type of material burning, whether it be a burning dump, grass fire, trees or tires.

The observers occupied the towers from April 1 through the end of October. This time frame was the season most likely to have conditions ideal for possible fires. In both late spring and early fall, the forest floors are carpeted with dried grasses and leaves. Spring/fall conditions such as hot, dry temperatures and high winds create ideal opportunities for forest fires.

Prior to the building of the first Adirondack fire tower, there were frequent outbreaks of serious fires that consumed huge acres of valuable Adirondack forest and killed its wildlife, fish and vegetation. On one occasion in September 1908, as acres of Adirondack forest burned out of control, smoke from these raging fires drifted south 250 miles, reaching lower Manhattan in New York City.

Most responsible for the fires were the lumbering industry, locomotives, campers, smokers and farmers. When the lumbering industry clear-cut the trees, it left behind bark and branches. As the bark and branches dried, they became tinder, very susceptible to catching fire. Trains powered by coal engines would spew hot embers from their smokestacks, igniting the dried tinder. Other causes of forest fires included careless campers leaving behind unattended campfires. Additionally, farmers clearing land for crops had to cut trees, generally burning the remaining limbs and brush. These burns could get out of control, setting ablaze the surrounding forest.

As the public became aware of fire prevention practices, the lumbering industry damped its practice of clear-cutting trees and vehicle roads replaced Adirondack Railroad travel, the need for tower observers lessened. In the early 1970s, the practice of air surveillance started to replace the need for fire towers. It was discovered to be less expensive to use the air pilot surveillance, which would fly in special flight patterns, covering a larger forested area. One air surveillance flight could cover the area previously patrolled by four tower observers. Today, though not used as initially intended, the trails to the remaining assembled twenty-five fire towers have become favorite destinations for hikers. Local clubs or associations maintain these towers, the observer cabins and the trails to their summits. The remaining towers, unfortunately, have either been dissembled or are currently privately owned, which means there is no public access.

SPOTLIGHT ON: OLYMPIC VILLAGE

Olympic Village in the town of Lake Placid, New York, played host for the winter Olympic games in 1932 and again in 1980. The first inhabits of the area originally known as North Elba came from the nearby New England states of Vermont and Connecticut. Following the Revolutionary

Lake Placid hosted the 1932 and 1980 Winter Olympics. The first ski jump, built in 1917, used only the hillside as the jump's surface.

War, tales of the Adirondacks having unlimited supplies of timber, iron, silver, wildlife, rich soils and majestic scenery caused droves of settlers across Lake Champlain to settle the unfamiliar New York woods. The first known settler was a Vermonter and Revolutionary War veteran, Elijah Bennet. With his wife, Rebecca, Elijah came in 1800, purchasing 292 acres around the present-day Mirror Lake shores.

In ten years, the North Elba settlement grew to more than two hundred people. In that time, Archibald McIntyre built the Elba Iron Works, only to be abandoned seven years later. The closing of the mine, along with the summer of

1816, which saw snow and ice in July and August, triggered many residents to abandon the area.

The 1840s saw the arrival of North Elba's most historical resident, John Brown. Brown was asked to come to North Elba to oversee wealthy abolitionist landowner Gerrit Smith's African American settlement.

Resort Town

Lake Placid's next phase of popularity came in what was known as the golden age of resorts. In that time, numerous inns and resorts were built to house, feed and entertain summer visitors. Prior to the Civil War and increasing from then on, the North Elba area attracted travelers, mostly painters, writers, sportsmen and nature lovers who wished to take in the high peaks landscape.

Stage Is Set as an Olympic Venue

In 1890, Melvin Dewey, creator and publisher of the Dewey Decimal System, came to North Elba, by then an already popular tourist destination. Dewey wanted a summer retreat for his family and intellectual friends. By 1895, he had his private social and recreational resort, with thirty-five members on 5 acres and 1 building. By 1904, Dewey's Lake Placid Club had begun hosting winter sporting events. For the first time, people traveled to Lake Placid for winter vacation to ski, skate, snowshoe and enjoy all sorts of winter outdoor play. By 1923, Lake Placid Club had grown to 9,600 acres with 356 buildings. Colleges came to use the resort to compete in winter sporting events. Melvin's son Godfred approached the Olympic Committee and was able to convince them that Lake Placid had the facilities, as well as the experience in hosting winter recreational events. For eleven days in February 1932, spectators and athletes gathered at the little village of Lake Placid, where fourteen Winter Olympic events occurred, including the bobsleigh, figure skating, ice hockey, cross-country skiing, Nordic combine, ski jumping and speed skating. Forty-eight years later, in 1980, Lake Placid would host another winter games.

SPOTLIGHT ON: XIV ARTICLE OF THE NEW YORK STATE CONSTITUTION

XIV Article of the New York State Constitution states: "The lands of the State…shall be forever kept as wild forest lands. They shall not be leased, sold, or exchanged, nor shall the timber thereon be sold, removed or destroyed." New York State voters passed this law on November 6, 1894. The law provides legal protection to the lands owned by the state within the Adirondack Park blue line from future logging or development to remain in their natural state.

In the years following the Revolutionary War, the government sold large areas of Adirondack forestlands for

84

Beavers started to dam this little stream flowing into Piseco Lake. Above is the bridge on Old Piseco Road.

pennies per acre to pay off war debts. Logging companies purchased most of these lands to supply a growing nation's thirst for lumber, aiding in the U.S. quest for Manifest Destiny. Iron companies purchased land for the iron ore beds but also needed the local wood for charcoal to fuel their vast blast furnaces. Leather companies desired hemlock to tan hides. Smaller softwoods were slashed and ground to make pulp. What remained, following the clear-cutting, was dry tinder and exposed barren soil now unable to retain moisture from the abundant snowfall and rains.

During the late 1800s, fires raged across the Adirondacks and other New England areas. Vacationers traveling through the Adirondacks saw the hideous scarring left behind. Public fears of widespread fires, erosion and depleted water supplies piloted the idea for Adirondack Park protection.

The conservation interest saw the Adirondack region as a huge sponge retaining the area's yearly abundant precipitation. The forest was seen as a huge sun-blocking canopy restricting evaporation. Both the forest canopy and mossy groundcover slowly released the yearly precipitation while maintaining a steady flow of water to the area's bogs, rivers and lakes. In allowing the clear-cutting of trees, ground exposed to wind and sun allowed for rapid evaporation of groundwater. All the Adirondack streams and lakes eventually feed New York City's drinking water supply.

Officials were also concerned with preserving an ample water supply for New York's Erie and Champlain Canal systems. New York State and especially New York City's economic livelihood relied heavily on canal commerce. Again, the Adirondack forest was believed to maintain a consistent and adequate water level for the canals.

Assisted by public outcry and expert testimony by Verplanck Colvin, preservationists looked to bring an end to the Adirondack devastation. In 1894, the people of New York State were able to legislatively secure the naturalness of the area by creating the Adirondack Park Preserve to be "forever wild."

Fun Activity!

Word Search: Adirondack Mountains

```
E T A G I V A N N K P N I D
N Y G P L T H O G O N O C S N
W O L N S A I R M I I E O O A
A U I E I T C I A T T T N L L
P D R T A H N I A A O I S A T
K O V V A E S V E V U L U T E
F C E E R T R I T R R O M I W
Y L O A N E S C F E I D P O C
E B L L S T N E S S S O T N I
V S O E M I U O R N M E I O L
R W R G T E R R K O C H O I L
U P X X S T H R E C F T N S Y
S S E N R E D L I W D E W O D
A B O L I T I O N I S T D R I
M O U N T A I N S B E A V E R
```

ABOLITIONIST	FISHING	NAVIGATE
ADVENTURE	FOREST	PRESERVATION
BEAVER	GLACIER	PULP
BOGS	HEMLOCK	RESORT
CONSERVATION	IDYLLIC	SURVEY
CONSUMPTION	IRON	THEODOLITE
DEFORESTATION	ISOLATION	TOURISM
ELEVATION	LYE	WETLAND
EROSION	MINERALS	WILDERNESS
EXTINCT	MOUNTAINS	

Chapter 6

Uniquely Adirondack

A little less than two hundred miles directly north of the George Washington Bridge in New York City, one of the most densely populated areas in the United States is an isolated wilderness jewel of six million acres called the Adirondack State Park. The park is a unique environmental experiment of both public and private wilderness lands. It is a prototype for the coexistence of human population in a designated wild space. Unlike the national park model, in the Adirondacks people live in the park amid wildlife, wetlands, forest, streams, lakes and mountains. The landscape is breathtaking as the seasonal colors nudge their presence along the woodlands. Sunsets present vivid oranges, violets and crimsons splashed across the horizon. At moments like these, one can almost unlock a doorway to one's own spiritual experiences. Sitting lakeside on a late afternoon offers a hypnotizing solitude as the sun glitters its blinding reflection across the water and ricochets its rhythmical presence. These moments we capture in our hearts and return to often in the winter months that follow.

The Adirondacks exhibit an impressive résumé of beauty. For years, its splendor has enticed artists, photographers and vacationers wanting to experience the nineteenth-century American dream about the wilderness. Enthusiastic travelers blindly followed the Adirondack guides deep into the backwoods. It was a time when in the United States the Industrial Revolution had taken over. People wanted to experience America as it was before that time. They came

Above: Fourth of July fireworks as part of the weekend Speculator celebration. The parade is held at 7:00 p.m., followed by the firemen's fair and then fireworks at 9:00 p.m. at the public beach.

Opposite: Ausable Chasm features self-guided rim-walk tours, rafting and tubing.

from long distances by train, carriage and boat to hunt, fish, sit by a nighttime campfire, sleep under the open sky or capture the last bit of wilderness on a canvas or in a photograph. They gathered together to share stories of the past while disclosing their hopes for the future.

SPOTLIGHT ON: TOURIST TRAVEL

One of the first groups of summer visitors to use the Adirondacks as a getaway retreat were artists. The allure of the Adirondack forests, mountains and lakes and the artists' general desire to capture nature's attractions brought New York City painters here. Upon returning to the city, their portraits were displayed by popular galleries in art exhibitions, where the rich and educated viewed their works. **Roswell Morse Shurtleff** (1838–1915) was one of the earliest and best-known watercolor painters displaying the Keene Valley and Ausable River region. Additionally, writers came, like **William Murray**, who published *Adventures in the Wilderness* in 1869. The book recounts his Adirondack hunting, boating and fishing experiences, and it ultimately fascinated the wealthy. **Seneca Ray Stoddard**, early Adirondack photographer born in 1844 in Wilton, New York, is best known for his nineteenth-century photographs, writings and illustrations representing life in the Adirondack wilderness. His book *The Adirondacks Illustrated*, published in 1874, is a literary travel guide complete with etchings illustrating the Adirondacks' most beautiful landscapes, gentle lakes and welcoming accommodations. In this guidebook, Stoddard describes various towns' histories, people, featured local attractions and transportation schedules for boat and stage and suggests guides to hire whose specialty might be fishing, hunting or traversing a

The Hayes family spends the day at Frontier Town in 1980, watching the water wheel power the old mill.

scenic mountain trail. Stoddard's photographs and textual accounts of the Adirondacks are credited with promoting travel and making it a little less difficult in an otherwise unknown Adirondack wilderness. Weekly articles in the *New York Times* gave accounts of socialites' adventures in destinations like Paul Smith's Hotel, world-renowned for its backwoods entertainment and lodging. Other popular destinations were Blue Mountain Lake and Lake Placid. The Lake Placid Club was the first to offer four-season vacationing.

The difficulty in travel in the early years did not seem to be a distraction, as those who did make the trip were granted a certain amount of bragging rights for having the rugged, enduring character to make the voyage. Transportation in those days was often by some combination of carriage, stagecoach, steamboat and railroad. It wasn't until the 1920s that the first automobile traversed the primitive dirt or clapboard roads.

In the 1940s, the family theme amusement park was born. The North Pole, home of Santa's Work Shop, first opened in 1949 on the base of Whiteface Mountain. Frontier Town followed in 1952; the park's theme was the American Wild West. Frontier Town closed in 1998. In 1954, businessman Charles Wood opened Story Town in Queensbury, a Mother Goose nursery rhyme theme park. Today, Story Town has undergone huge changes and is presently the Great Escape, a Six Flags theme park. The Enchanted Forest in Old Forge opened in 1956 as a storybook theme park featuring Paul Bunyan. Over the years, the Enchanted Forest made expansion efforts to compete with the larger parks, including water rides as a main attraction.

Today's visitors seep in around Memorial Day, opening their camps in preparation for the summer months ahead. At the local grocery store, you will find more out-of-state license plates than those from New York. People from Massachusetts, New Hampshire and New Jersey steadily buy lakefront Adirondack summer homes. Usually after Labor Day, the summer visitors retreat from their three-month Adirondack residency.

Spotlight On: Guides

In 1893, the Forest Commission Report listed 626 licensed **guides**. Guides were the catalyst that opened up the region's most secluded areas to tourists. Newspapers and sporting magazines gave the Adirondacks much attention, featuring the area as the last great frontier for adventurers who enjoyed pleasure, health and relaxation. The rich, educated and artistic, as well as the average, appeared almost overnight to delight in the Adirondacks. However, the area's inaccessibility required local experts to provide navigational direction. Guides provided their parties with assistance to locate the best spots for fishing, hunting or the most spectacular views. Each guide brought his or her own unique guiding qualities and personality. No two were alike. Some were better than others at cooking, trapping, fishing, tending fires, mountain hiking, building shelters or storytelling.

Three of the most sought-after Adirondack guides from the mid-1800s to the 1900s were Alva Dunning, Orson Schofield Phelps and Mitchell Sabattis. Alva Dunning

Guides at Holland House, Blue Mountain Lake, 1885. *Courtesy of the Adirondack Room, Saranac Lake Free Library, Copy and Reuse Restrictions Apply.*

was known as the hermit guide of Raquette Lake. He was born in Lake Pleasant, and he disliked neighbors, the civilized world and modern progress. His enjoyment came from total isolation, but he would guide and take money from intruding travelers. As a natural born hunter, Dunning killed his first moose at age eleven. He had a total objection for game laws that attempted to restrict hunting to certain times of the year, as well as the number of animals shot per person. In one season, Dunning killed over one hundred moose. He believed, as did many other Adirondack people, that a man of the woods ought to be able to hunt, trap and fish whenever he needed the meat for food. He felt the game laws should only apply to the wasteful vacationers who often left behind the meat, taking only the trophy antlers.

Orson Schofield Phelps, better known as Old Man Phelps, was a different kind of guide who sought the woods for its beauty. As a boy, he helped his father survey the area and acquired an admiring respect for the Adirondack scenery. His love of nature and poetic way made him a favorite guide among many intellectuals. He easily traversed mountain trails, eager to show his group the area's sunsets, mountains or seasonal spectaculars. He especially favored Mount Marcy, having climbed to its summit over one hundred times. His exterior appearance revealed him

A kayak adventure entering Piseco Lake. See the mountain and cloud reflection on the quiet waters.

having "no use for soap, comb, or razor and whose clothes seem to have been put on years ago."

Mitchell Sabattis of the Long Lake area was a pureblooded Abenaki Indian. He was known as a gently honest man who devoted his life to both his family and the Long Lake Methodist Church. Mitchell raised money to build the church and, after its completion, often preached there. He had a great skill of woodcraft. In the winter months, he and his sons built Adirondack guide boats known for their easy and quiet rowing qualities. As a guide, he was a favorite among tourists for his trapping and hunting skills. He was able to follow the tracks of any animal in daylight or dusk. Through the years, he and his family had great success guiding and hosting summer vacationers at their Long Lake resort.

SPOTLIGHT ON: CONSUMPTION

Consumption was a term used in the 1800s for the widespread disease tuberculosis, also called TB. It was called consumption as it seemed to destroy, or consume, the body from within. The disease affects the lungs, and symptoms include an extended cough, accompanying chest pain, fever, chills, loss of appetite, weight loss, swollen neck glands, paling skin color and coughing blood. Tuberculosis is caused by slow-growing aerobic bacteria and is spread when the infected person coughs, sneezes or spits active disease aerosol droplets into the air. Consumption was considered a socioeconomic disease associated with poor city living conditions, including poorly ventilated and crowed apartments, polluted drinking water and streets covered in animal waste, garbage and filth.

In 1870, Dr. Edward Livingston Trudeau, himself stricken with tuberculosis, traveled to his friend Paul Smith's

Trudeau sanitarium patients "curing" in winter, children's infirmary. *Courtesy of the Adirondack Room, Saranac Lake Free Library, Copy and Reuse Restrictions Apply.*

Dr. Edward Trudeau, physician, established treatment facilities in Saranac Lake. He dedicated his life to treating and researching tuberculosis, a disease that at one time killed one in seven people in the United States.

hotel to die. In the days to follow, however, Dr. Trudeau, embraced by the clear, crisp wilderness air, surprisingly recovered. Was it the Adirondack life and clean mountain air that eased his pulmonary condition?

Fifteen years later, Dr. Trudeau opened "Little Red," a small consumption cure cottage in Saranac Lake. Trudeau's Adirondack cottage sanitarium was tailored for the infected poor, those financially unable to afford the lavish European sanitariums. Starting as a small wilderness TB treatment center, the success of the Saranac Lake sanitarium became well known, and it eventually attracted the nation's best doctors, researchers and popular patients of the time, such as author Robert Louis Stevenson and magician Harry Houdini.

Trudeau did not know the cure for TB but could effectively treat its symptoms with a routine of rest; patient isolation;

sunlight; non-taxing work; wholesome, hearty meals; and outdoor leisure in all weather conditions. Trudeau believed the clear balsam mountain air was a crucial element in treatment. He also carefully selected his patients, restricting admittance to younger candidates in the initial stages of the disease, believing both to be criteria for a successful recovery. Another factor in the effective treatment of TB was contributed to the geographical isolation of Saranac Lake. The inaccessibility of the Adirondacks did not allow large populations to either enter or leave the small village, therefore restricting exposure to stronger strains of the disease.

Antibiotics discovered in 1946 proved to be an effective drug treatment against tuberculosis. The Saranac Lake tuberculosis sanitarium treated over fifteen thousand patients. But with the discovery of the drug treatment Trudeau's sanitarium, along with others, became obsolete, economically crippling the little Adirondack village. The journey from wilderness to worldwide renowned fame would relapse to wilderness.

Spotlight On: Yarns

The dictionary definition of a **yarn** is a long, often elaborate narrative of real or fictitious adventures. An Adirondack yarn was a way in which people entertained. It was how news was spread and how each generation learned about family members, the people they knew and the places where

People at camp, 1903. These popular three-sided lean-to structures were the shelter of choice for most guides. *Courtesy of the Library of Congress.*

they lived. Yarns tell about Adirondack adventures but also can transport you back into the life of backwoodsmen as they logged, trapped, fished, hunted, farmed and guided. Some yarns taught adults and children lessons about life or how they should conduct themselves. Most Adirondack yarn spinning was done around an evening campfire or a parlor stove or at a local tavern.

One Sunday, a minister told us an Adirondack story relating to the importance of attending church and being part of that church community. Once there was an older widowed farmer living in North Elba, New York, taking care of his crops and animals all by himself. In late spring, the farmer, seemingly overburdened with his farm tasks,

A day's vacation to Frontier Town interrupted by a train robbery! How much loot will they take today?

decided not to attend church. Rather, he would pray and give thanks for his life during his work. After a while, word spread to members of the church, including the minister, that farmer George would not be attending church. Folks in the church community talked about how he would be missed, as he had a warm smile and a gentle way of conversation. Later in the season, on a fall evening, the pastor drove his horse and carriage to visit the farmer to see how he was doing. Farmer George welcomed the pastor, offering him coffee and some leftover cornbread from that night's supper. They sat around the kitchen coal stove discussing the weather, hunting, fishing and this year's crop. After a while, the preacher took the coal iron pincher hanging on the brick wall and grasped a piece of coal from the intense blazing group of coal pieces heaped in the middle of the stove's coal box. He removed that piece from its glowing cluster, placing it by itself on the brick floor near the stove. Both the farmer and the preacher watched the solitary piece of coal slowly lose its bright radiance. Neither said a word for a long time; they just watched that piece of coal lose its glimmer in the absence of the other pieces. Eventually, the farmer turned to the preacher and said, "Well, I'll see you in church next Sunday." Without saying a direct word, the preacher showed the farmer how he needed the church, the church community needed him and being part of that community keeps his flame burning.

Fun Activity!

Listening for Nature

- Select a sampling area to listen for sounds (lake shore, forest, stream, open field).
- Measuring instrument: Tape recorder or your own good hearing (ears), along with a piece of paper.
- Describe and write down the specifics of your sample area for recording, including date, time, weather conditions, location, topography, vegetation (evergreens/hardwoods), elevation, season, wind direction, air temperature, etc.
- Data collection type: If you have a tape recorder, you may want to record nature sounds, but better yet, just close your eyes and focus on listening to the sounds you hear and distinguish whether they are natural or man-made.
- Overview: Natural sounds are essential to the Adirondack Park ecosystem. Nature's acoustic environment reveals its importance in several ways:
  - It is how animal species communicate.
  - It can be a form of mating and courtship.
  - It can be how animals tell the findings of water, food and a safe habitat.
  - It is used to warn others of predators and weather changes.
  - It is used to protect their young.

- Goals: By listening to the sounds of nature, we will be able to:
  - o Distinguish between man-made sounds and natural sounds.
  - o Acquire a desire to preserve a quiet Adirondack State Park.
- Pre-listening Activity: Sources of Sounds
  - o Think about the sounds of chainsaw, church bells, garbage truck, school bus, motorboat, etc.
  - o Think about the sound a robin makes before the rain, woodpecker, flock of Canada geese, waterfall, etc.

Activity: Find your sampling area to sit and record with tablet of paper or below chart. Close your eyes and listen for sounds for fifteen minutes. Record them based on the category of man-made or natural sounds.

At another time, return to the sampling area and repeat the process. Note the differences in the sounds. Reflect on why the sounds have changed. Are there more man-made v. natural sounds based on the time of day?

- Does weather change the mix of sounds? Compare sounds from morning, noon and evening.
- Amplitude is the sound strength, or what we call volume or loudness. Which sounds were louder?
- Frequency is the number of times the sound is heard. Which sounds were most frequently heard?
- How might vegetation and topography contribute to our sound experience?
- Brainstorm ways to minimize (intrusive sound sources) man-made sounds in the state park.

Sounds in a Habitat Worksheet

	Natural Sounds	**Man-made Sounds**
Wildlife:	Bird	
	_____	_____
	_____	_____
	_____	_____
	_____	_____
	_____	_____
	_____	_____
Water:	Rain	_____
	_____	_____
	_____	_____
	_____	_____
	_____	_____
	_____	_____

Fun Activity!

Crossword Puzzle: Adirondack State Park

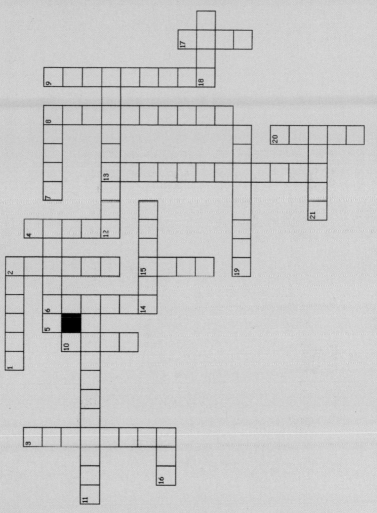

Weather: Thunder   _____

             _____   _____

             _____   _____

             _____   _____

Vegetation: Leaves blowing across   _____
             pavement

             _____   _____

             _____   _____

             _____   _____

             _____   _____

Date
Time
Weather condition
Place recorded
Topography
Vegetation
Season
Wind direction
Air temperature
Elevation